MiM Mini Guide No.5:

Interwar Industrial Architecture

Joshua Abbott

MiM Mini Guide No.5: Interwar Industrial Architecture

Published in the United Kingdom 2024 by Mod in Metro Publishing

www.modernism-in-metroland.co.uk

Words, Photographs and Design by Joshua Abbott

Printed by Mixam Ltd, Watford

ISBN: 978-1-7396857-4-4

Interwar Industrial Architecture in London and the Suburbs

The 1920s and 30s were a golden era of industrial design in Britain. The building of the new arterial roads around London allowed manufacturers to move out from the crowded inner city and establish newly built premises in the growing suburbs. Connections to roads such as the Great West, Western Avenue and Great Cambridge could link these factories to central London and elsewhere, allowing raw materials to be delivered (sometimes by rail or canal) and finished products to be collected for distribution. The placement of factories next to these roads also influenced their design. Instead of inward looking buildings in cramped urban areas, the new industrial buildings could be more expressive, advertising their wares and creating a dynamic, modern brand image.

Up to this point, industrial buildings such as factories were often built as huge, brick edifices with rows of half moon windows, or designed to look like oversized Greek temples, with grand doric columns. The emergence of modernism and art deco during the early part of the 20th century was largely ignored by British architects, who preferred to look back to the past for influence. The designers of industrial buildings, who occupied almost the lowest rung on the ladder of architectural respectability, took to these new styles with much more eagerness, using the functionality of modernism and the mix and match spirit of art deco to produce a new form of industrial architecture.

Foremost amongst these firms was that of Wallis Gilbert and Partners, formed by Thomas Wallis in 1916 with the aim of designing and building factories in partnership with US firm Trussed Concrete Steel Ltd (Truscon). Over the next 25 years the firm would design well over 100 factories and other industrial buildings. They were initially influenced by the American Daylight style factories, built with a concrete frame and featuring floor to ceiling windows for maximum floor space and illumination. The style of their factory buildings evolved from this basic mode towards what became known as the Fancy style, with frontages in elaborate designs hiding the more prosaic factory buildings behind and also advertising the company's wares. These 'Fancy' buildings like the Hoover Factory and Firestone Factory would become fixtures of the arterial roads, landmarks to measure a tedious car journey.

The other prominent designer of industrial buildings of the era was engineer turned architect Owen Williams. Williams also worked for Truscon before coming to fame with his work on the 1924 British Empire Exhibition at Wembley, where amongst other buildings, he helped create the Palace of Industry, an exhibition hall intended to showcase British industry. Williams' best known factories are the Boots buildings in Beeston, a collection of pioneering concrete and glass structures built between 1930-38. He designed a few other factory buildings, mostly now demolished, but is represented in this guide by his extension to the Hunt Partners Factory in Clapton.

Of course there were other firms and individuals that designed factories and industrial buildings in the interwar years. These include lesser known names like Fuller, Hall and Foulsham, Hal Williams and Company, Nicholas and Dixon-Spain and Harry Courteneay Constantine, as well as more prestigious architects who occasionally turned their hand to industrial commissions such as Giles Gilbert Scott and Bannister Fletcher. In general these buildings proved more popular with the person in the street than in the architectural press, with Nikolas Pevsner famously calling the Hoover Factory " perhaps the most offensive of the modernistic atrocities along this road typical of the by-pass factories". Thomas Wallis was quite honest about the commercial aspect of his designs, telling the RIBA in 1933 that " A little money spent on something to focus the attention of the public is not money wasted but a good advertisement".

The golden age of factory building came to an end with the outbreak of war in 1939. Afterwards, a new sobriety took hold of architectural design, with material and manpower seriously depleted. Many factories had been damaged in the Blitz, and those that survived saw many companies move manufacturing to the New Towns built in the immediate postwar years like Stevenage and Basildon, and eventually abroad. Developers quickly demolished many of these defunct factories, with the most famous case being the Firestone factory on the Great West Road Brentford. Opened in 1928 for the tyre company, and designed in a grand deco style by Wallis, Gilbert and Partners, it was hastily demolished over August Bank Holiday in 1980 as the paperwork to protect it lay in an in-tray at the Dept of the Environment.

The destruction of the Firestone Factory prompted a wave of anger, and was the impetus for a greater protection of interwar and industrial buildings. However, many more had already been and would eventually be demolished. Some of the most significant of these include; the Guinness Brewery in Park Royal (1936) by Giles Gilbert Scott, the Allom Brothers Factory in Morden (1937) by Stanley Hall Easton & Robertson, the Sainsbury's Warehouse and Factory, Blackfriars (1934) by Owen Williams, the Lovell & Christmas Warehouse in Smithfield (1937) by Joseph Hill, and many, many others.

This mini guide aims to document some of the survivors of the interwar years, covering factories and their associated offices, workshops, warehouses, power stations and other industrial buildings. It is arranged moving from the North West of the capital in a clockwise fashion right back around to the West, exploring buildings in geographical groups often located next to a prominent road.

References and Further Reading

David Cottam Sir Owen Williams (1890-1969) Works Architectural Association Publications 1986

Bridget Cherry & Nikolaus Pevsner Buildings of England London 3: North West Yale University Press 1991

Joan Skinner Form and Fancy: Factories and Factory Buildings by Wallis, Gilbert & Partners 1916-39 Liverpool University Press 1997

The Works- Factories in London 1918-39 Parts 1&2 Jon Bolter AA Files 36 & 37 1998

Bridget Cherry & Nikolaus Pevsner Buildings of England London 4: North Yale University Press 1998

Bridget Cherry, Charles O'Brien & Nikolaus Pevsner Buildings of England London 2: South Yale University Press 2002

Bridget Cherry, Charles O'Brien & Nikolaus Pevsner Buildings of England London 5: East Yale University Press 2004

James Bettley, Nikolaus Pevsner & Bridget Cherry Buildings of England Hertfordshire Yale University Press 2019

North West London

The construction of Western Avenue began in 1921, connecting central London to Buckinghamshire and beyond. Like the other arterial roads created during the same period it became a prime area for factory building. Most prominent among those built is the **Hoover Factory** by Wallis Gilbert and Partners, constructed from 1932, with ten separate buildings making up the site. The two buildings facing onto the road are the most interesting, and not by coincidence, the only survivors of the original plan. The 220ft long office block was designed in 1931, its facade finished in generous glazing and coloured tilework. At either end are two staircase towers with quarter moon windows inspired by the work of Erich Mendelsohn. The main entrance doorway is spectacular, a riot of colour and patterns, designed to impress visitors and passers-by alike. Hoover left the building in the 1980's, with Tesco taking over the and converting the rear into a supermarket and letting out offices in the front. The main block has now been converted into apartments.

Hoover Factory

Hoover Factory, Perivale

A little further west on the busy road is the **Aladdin Lamps Factory**, from 1931. It was designed by the partnership of C. Nicholas and J.E. Dixon-Spain, for the American company, one of many built during the period for U.S. businesses after a general tariff of 10% was imposed on most imported goods. The design of the factory is fairly simple with a two-storey, steel-framed brick front building with a tower above the entrance. The factory buildings were set behind with angled skylights to provide illumination for the shop floor. The factory was initially built amongst the fields of Greenford, with Western Avenue arriving on its doorstep in 1937. The factory closed in 1972 and the site was eventually converted into a retail store with the rear buildings demolished.

Not directly on Western Avenue, but near enough to provide easy access, are a few other factory buildings. In Greenford is the former **Glaxo Building**, completed in 1935 to designs by Wallis, Gilbert & Partners. The scheme included a headquarters for the newly formed Glaxo Laboratories company, with research and production facilities behind. The front range repeats the plan used with the Hoover factory and other Wallis Gilbert & Partners factories, in having a prestigious office block placed in front of functional production buildings. The Glaxo office building was set out in an aircraft plan, with two long wings coming off a central hall and entrance, The two storey building is built in sand lime brick around a steel frame, and features horizontal ranges of windows with black acrylic panels between them. Glaxo occupied the building until 2009, when they moved to Stockley Park. The site was developed into housing with the Grade II listed office block kept intact.

Aladdin Lamps Factory

Glaxo Factory, Greenford

North West London

To the north at Wembley is the **Wrigley's Factory**, a first commission from an American client for Wallis, Gilbert & Partners, when they asked the partnership to design a factory building on a plot of land near Kenton station. The original building was a four storey factory built in reinforced concrete using the Truscon system with mushroom columns supporting each floor from below. This meant more space could be used for glazing on the side walls, providing greater illumination to the shop floor. Wallis, Gilbert and Partners added a couple of extensions to the building over the next 30 years including the attached four storey block to the east. Wrigley's relocated to Plymouth in 1970 and the building was converted into smaller offices.

Close proximity to the North Circular saw industrial estates spring up at Park Royal, Neasden and Stonebridge Park. Many of the buildings put up on these estates were smaller versions of the grander "bypass factories" like the Hoover and Glaxo, with a deco style front and functional rear. On Beresford Avenue, Stonebridge Park is something slightly different, the former **Rizla Factory** (1937) by Harry Courtenay Constantine, which is a wedge-shaped building with a circular drum entrance. Other, later, neighbouring industrial buildings have been cleared for a large housing development, with the former factory surviving for now. One of the most written about factory buildings in the architectural press of the 1930s was the *Electroflo Factory*, Park Royal (1937) by Adie, Button & Partners. The six storey building took obvious inspiration from continental modernism, with its reinforced concrete walls and long rows of glazing. The structure still survives, now known as Unimix House and covered in silver cladding.

Wrigley's Factory, Wembley

The central areas of London had been home to numerous industrial buildings and factories before the construction of the arterial roads, and many companies opted to remain there. The outer edges of Camden and Islington were home to manufacturing buildings with the most well known and eye-catching being the **Carreras Cigarette Factory** in Mornington Crescent. It was built from 1926 on a strip of land previously used as a communal garden, a fact that would shape its form; a 550 foot long block that sits between Hampstead Road and Mornington Crescent. Designed by brothers M.E. & O.H. Collins with A.G. Porri, the building is decorated in colourful Egyptian-themed detailing, including repeated black cat reliefs in between the giant papyriform columns and two large cats outside the entrance. All of this decoration is a replacement, with the original being stripped in the 1960s, when it was converted to office use.

Designed in an altogether more serious tone was the modernist **Gilbey House** (1937), a complex featuring a factory, offices and warehouse, for the gin distilling company on Jamestown Road, Camden Town. Its designers were the impeccably modernist architects Eric Mendelsohn and Serge Chermayeff, working together briefly during Mendelsohn's flight from Germany to the U.S. via Britain. They added an extension to a building from 1894, extending the premises with a reinforced concrete structure, engineered by Felix Samuely, which sits on cork insulated foundations, designed to lessen vibrations from the nearby trainline.

Carreras Cigarette Factory, Mornington Crescent

Gilbey House, Camden Town

Some companies wanted to be as close to the shopping areas of Oxford Street and Bond Street as possible, able to fulfil orders from department stores quickly. Fitzrovia is home to a few buildings that reflect its importance as an area of industry, particularly for the garment trade. On Great Titchfield Street is **Elsley House & Court** (1936-37), a speculative development of small units built to let to garment firms who didn't have the means to move further out or build their own premises. The architects Waite and Waite designed the building as a seven storey block, decorated with art deco details and featuring a staircase tower. Opposite is **Circus House** (1936), intended for a similar purpose, and designed by Harry Courtenay Constantine with a glazed staircase tower.

On Cleveland Street is **Middlesex House** (1936) a modernist five storey warehouse designed by A.D. Clare. The building was later used as a factory before being converted into offices by John McAslan and Partners in 2001, now home to Make Architects. On Capper Street, just off Tottenham Court Road, is another Waite and Waite building, **Shropshire House** (1932), a large warehouse which balances modernist functionalism with art deco touches, such as the cloud-like balconies. It also has a thin, tall entrance on Tottenham Court Road with projecting metal windows. Waite and Waite were responsible for a number of speculative commercial developments in central London, and consisted of the architect Donald M. Waite and his two sons Douglas and Archibald. Another bold modernist design is the former offices to the **Robert Rigby Ltd**. factory on Northington Street. The company manufactured cinematography equipment, both here and in Birmingham, and the surviving building has horizontal rows of metal framed windows and an indented corner.

Elsley House, Great Titchfield Street

Circus House, Great Titchfield Street

Middlesex House, Cleveland Street

Shropshire House, Capper Street

Robert Rigby Ltd, Northington Street

Clerkenwell

The areas of Clerkenwell and Farringdon have a rich history of printing, with a number of printworks built in the area in the interwar years. In **Summers Street**, just off Clerkenwell Road, is a former printworks and warehouse from 1933 by Stanley Peach, better known for being the designer of the Centre Court at Wimbledon. The five storey building is built in rendered brick around a steel frame with concrete floor bands, and large areas of glazing. It was converted to apartments in 1992, with architect Piers Gough drawing up a plan for 23 apartments in the building.

On Bowling Green Lane is the former *Temple Press* (1938-9), a printworks built for Temple Press Ltd, a publisher of specialist and technical journals, including a wide array on motoring. Designed by F.W. Troup & H.R. Steele with a reinforced concrete frame, the six storey building curves around the corner of Bowling Green Lane and Northampton Road, with bands of glazing running the length of the building. The building is now home to the London Metropolitan Archives.

Former Printworks, Summers Street

Clerkenwell

A short walk away on Aylesbury Street is *Woodbridge House*, built as speculative factory units from 1936-39, designed by the firm of Fuller, Hall and Foulsham. It is a wedge-shaped, five storey building in brick with bands of white render, metal framed windows and a tall staircase tower. Also by Fuller, Hall and Foulsham is the former *Falk Stadelmann Warehouse* on Saffron Hill from 1937. Falk Stadelmann were manufacturers of maps and light fittings who had moved to new premises on the corner of Clerkenwell Road and Farringdon Road in 1923, with a new building designed by Fuller, Horsey, Sons & Cassell, replacing a previous building destroyed in a Zeppelin air raid in 1917.

The 1937 warehouse was built in concrete with horizontal bands of windows and central staircase tower. The new building would also be the victim of German bombardment, being damaged by a V2 rocket in August 1944. The warehouse was rebuilt and later used as a printworks before being extended and converted into apartments, now known as the Ziggurat Building.

On the corner of Skinner Street and St John Street is the former **Ingersoll Warehouse and Showrooms**, designed in 1931 by Stanley Waghorn for the watch company. Similar to the other buildings mentioned in this area, it is built in brick with metal framed windows, and features green tilework on the upper levels with the company's name in mosaic. The building, now flats, was later used as a pattern factory by Vogue.

Ingersoll Warehouse, St John Street

The bane of many motorists' lives in outer London, the North Circular was built partially to allow better transport links for the newly built industrial premises that had moved out from the traditional manufacturing areas of East London in the interwar years. Just off the road at Wood Green is the former **Barratt's Chocolate Factory** on Clarendon Road. The confectionery company was founded in the mid-19th century, moving from Hoxton to Wood Green in 1880 to expand their facilities. Over the next 40 years various buildings were put up as the business saw both peaks and troughs.

From 1922, the partnership of Joseph Emberton and P.J. Westwood were employed to modernise the complex. They built a number of different buildings on the site over a 23 year period, beginning with the curved extension along Coburg Road. The most interesting part for us is the 1930s block to the rear of this, a purely modernist 5-storey structure in bright white render with metalwork balconies. The site closed down in 1980, and was eventually converted to use by small traders and artisans. The ceaseless demolition and building on the site continue to this day, with housing being built on the site.

Barratt's Chocolate Factory, Wood Green

The A10 or the Great Cambridge Road became an attractive area for factory building in the interwar years, with industrial building springing up in Ponders End and Edmonton. The **Ripaults Factory** is just off the Great Cambridge, on Southbury Road. It was opened in 1936, built for a company who produced cables and components for the automotive industry. The architect A.H. Durnford designed the building in a miniature version of the streamlined style of the other bypass factories found around the suburbs. The main building is a sleek two storey block, with ribbon windows and chrome strip decoration, and is currently home to Travis Perkins.

Further to the east, on Fulbourne Road in Walthamstow is an extension to the **ASEA Factory** from 1936. Now council offices, the structure was designed by Wallis, Gilbert & Partners and features a three storey block with horizontal ribbons of windows with a grand entrance at the southern end complete with large stone doorway. The factory produced large electrical transformers. The building was later bought by Fuller Electrical and then by Hawker Siddeley, as part of their large complex in Walthamstow, and are now council offices.

ASEA Factory, Walthamstow

The eastern side of the North Circular also attached a number of factory buildings, looking to take advantage of rapid transport of materials and goods. In the built up back streets of Forest Gate is the **Trebor Factory** in Katherine Road. It was built between 1935-7 to designs by the partnership of Higgins and Thomerson, for the confectionary company who had based themselves here since 1907. The new premises contained an electric production line, enabling them to produce their sweets faster and in greater volume. The factory was hit by the Luftwaffe in 1944 but rebuilt to continue production, eventually closing in 1981. The building has now been converted to apartments, maintaining the distinctive TREBOR QUALITY SWEETS sign on the exterior.

Also by Higgins and Thomerson is the former **Yardley Factory** in the High Street, Stratford (1937). Yardley had been in the area since 1905 with a factory on Carpenters Road, but new moderne premises were built in the mid-1930s. Nowadays it is apartments, but the main body of the factory survives, with its curved end, complete with its tiled panel of lavender pickers, and the rectangular block with long horizontal windows. In Clapton is the extension to the former **Hunt Partners Factory** in Grosvenor Way, used to manufacture packaging. It was added by Owen Williams in 1939, as a four storey extension, built with reinforced concrete cross frames, concrete floor slabs and in situ concrete walls, a great example of William's engineering knowledge. The building was turned into an aircraft factory during World War II and has now been renamed the De Havilland building and converted to flats.

Trebor Factory, Forest Gate

Yardely Factory, Stratford

Hunt Partners Factory, Clapton

The east end of London was traditionally a working class area with much in the way of industry and manufacturing. Remnants of this can still be found all around the neighbourhoods of Hackney and Tower Hamlets, now often converted into flats and creative workspaces. Along Commercial Street in Shoreditch is the large edifice of the **Godfrey Phillips Cigarette Factory**. The company had been in the area since 1865, starting with a shop before growing into a major manufacturer of tobacco products. The site was expanded from 1922 through until 1936. with B.W.H. Scott adding the art deco frontage with its tall clock tower and linking bridge to the adjacent showrooms.

A little further north on Shoreditch High Street is the **Tea Building**. It was built in 1933 by Hal Williams and Company, for the Lipton company, and was originally used as a bacon curing factory. By the end of that decade it was also used to pack and store tea, hence the current day name. It is a large building, eight storeys high, built in brick with art deco detailing. It was converted in 2001 into creative office spaces for start ups and the like by Allford Hall Monaghan Morris, who kept many of its original industrial features. In Spitalfields is *Brody House*, a former button and sequin factory from 1938. It was built for the Brody Trims company in a modernist style with white rendered walls and large areas of glazing. The building has now been converted to apartments and extensions added in a similar style.

Tea Building, Shoreditch High Street

Godfrey Phillips Cigarette Factory, Shoreditch High Street

Furnishing and Hardware Warehouse

A little further south is something quite different. It is the **Co-Operative Wholesale Society Warehouses and Offices** on Prescot Street and Leman Street. The group was built between 1930-39, and designed by the Society's in-house architect for London, Leonard Grey Ekins. Rather than modernist functionality or art deco flamboyance, Ekins opted for heavy brick Expressionism, influenced by 1920s Dutch and German architecture. The office facade is made up of tall brick piers divided by windows and bronze panels. The top of the building sports a mansard roof with green pantiles and moulded cornices. The entrances, on both Prescot St, Leman St and their junction, are heavy stone affairs with deco-like decoration.

Facing onto both Prescot Street and Chamber Street is the **Furnishing and Hardware Warehouse** of 1938, which uses the same, intricate brick style of its neighbour, The earlier, faience-clad Drapery Warehouse on Leman Street of 1929-30, was demolished in 2010.

Co-Operative Wholesale Society Warehouses and Offices

To the east, the area of Whitechapel was well known for its concentration of businesses associated with clothes manufacturing, or the 'Rag Trade' as it was also known. The area features a number of buildings reflecting this history. The most prominent of these is **Cheviot House**, on the junction of Commercial Road and Philpot Street. It was designed in 1937 by architect Goodman George Winbourne for the textile firm Kornberg and Segal. The six storey building has horizontal windows strips interspersed with rendered bands which terminate with a curve at the spectacular corner window which rises five floors to the top of the building. The building was only used as an industrial building until 1948, when it was bought by the then local authority, the Metropolitan Borough of Stepney. Plans to demolish Cheviot House in 2013 were fiercely fought and the building was converted into flats.

Just around the corner is the first of three factory buildings by Hume Victor Kerr, an architect who designed a number of buildings in this area including the streamlined Gwynne House (1938) apartments on Turner Street. *Comfort House* was a small clothing factory and showroom from 1932 for M.Levy. It has a miniature version of Cheviot House's corner window, as well as tall staircase towers at either end of the building. Under one of these towers is a doorway with WORKS ENTRANCE in projecting metal lettering.

Cheviot House

On New Road are two further factory buildings by Victor Kerr, **Service House** (1929-30) and *Empire House* (1934). Service House, now the New Road Hotel, was built as a clothing workshop and car park with a four storey steel framed building with lettable workshops to the road, and a three storey building to the rear with parking and more workshops. The building was part of the garment trade into the 1980s before falling into disrepair. It was then refurbished and opened as a hotel in 2018.

Empire House replaced a row of houses and workshops at the north of New Road, opening in 1934. Like Service House it was built with a steel frame surrounded by rendered brick with three horizontal window strips and prominent name sign. The building was renovated in 2019 and now contains office-workshops. Victor Kerr also designed the conjoined Commerce House and Industry House (1934) on Middlesex Street, with a streamlined facade that stretched along the block, sadly demolished in 1990.

Service House

South London has a strong industrial heritage, with many businesses basing themselves near the River Thames to collect goods brought in from all corners of the world. One of these was **Alaska Factory** (1932) on Grange Road in Bermondsey, another building by Wallis, Gilbert & Partners, this time for C.W. Martins & Sons. The seven-storey concrete structure replaced an earlier factory, known as the K building, used for processing Alaskan fur seal skins. The new building contained sections for drying, sorting and dyeing, as well as a laboratory and a sawdust store. In the 1980s the building was converted to office use and then a little later to apartments. The most eye-catching part of the exterior is the red "Alaska" sign, which originally said "Martins"

On a smaller scale is the *Sunlight Laundry* on Acre Lane, Brixton. Designed by architect F. E. Simpkins and opened in 1937, the building has a central entrance tower with two long wings either side, in a streamline moderne fashion. The Sunlight company offered laundry and drying services throughout the country, primarily for homes, and then later with the rise of the washing machine, for hotels, restaurants and other businesses. The building is now home to small offices.

Alaska Factory

On the south bank of the River Thames is one of London's most famous interwar industrial landmarks, **Battersea Power Station** (1929-55) at Nine Elms, with its distinctive four giant chimneys. The structure is actually two power stations, A and B, built over 16 years to appear as one building. It was constructed to replace a number of smaller power stations that had supplied electricity until that point. The initial design for the power station was undertaken by Leonard Pearce of the London Power Company, with J. Theo Halliday and Sir Giles Gilbert Scott responsible for making the raw industrial beast a bit more palatable. The building is constructed of brown Blockley brick around a steel frame, with a reinforced concrete roof. The four chimneys were constructed of precast concrete, and given the appearance of fluted Doric columns. The control room of station A was decorated by Halliday in a streamlined deco style, complete with marble walls and lighting set in a decorative steel frame.

The power station operated until October 1983, with the station's equipment becoming outdated. Then followed a long period of waiting as various proposals for its reuse or even demolition came and went. Eventually a redevelopment deal with a Malaysian conglomerate was agreed that saw the station conveyed to apartments and a shopping centre, which opened in 2022. As part of this, the chimneys were completely rebuilt as the originals had corroded with age and pollution. Giles Scott was also responsible for the design of another power station, Bankside, completed in 1963 and now home to the Tate Gallery.

Battersea Power Station

Further south in Croydon, Purley Way was home to a number of industrial buildings built on the expanses of the 1920 airport. One survivor is the former **National Aircraft Factory**, with its 1933 art deco facade by T. Graham Crump, hiding the original, functional 1918 buildings. The new frontage with its clocktower and streamlined windows was added to make it attractive for companies who wanted to relocate themselves to this area as the airfield was redeveloped after the First World War.

Just around the corner on Queensway is *Bourjois House*, originally built in 1939 to designs by Fuller, Hall and Foulsham, for the cosmetics company. The proximity to the airport was unfortunate for the building, with an aircraft colliding with it in the late 1930s, and then being hit by a Luftwaffe bomb during World War II. The factory was reconstructed and is still home to Bourjois today.

National Aircraft Factory, Purley Way

Great West Road

The most famous surviving concentration of the interwar factory can be found on the Great West Road in Brentford, known as the 'Golden Mile'. The road was officially opened on 30th May 1925, with King George V cutting a ceremonial ribbon. In the years that followed the land on either side of the new road became prime territory for businesses looking for extra space to expand production and make their products known.

The first major company to do this was the US company, *Firestone Tire & Rubber*, who built a factory on a 28 acre site in 1928. Wallis, Gilbert & Partners were commissioned to design the new building, with the partnership seen as understanding American industrial processes and requirements. As would become common for factory designs along the Great West Road and elsewhere, a spectacular art deco office block was built in front of humdrum production buildings, with the front building also acting as a giant billboard for the company. Firestone closed the factory in November 1979, with the site being bought by conglomerate Trafalgar House. When the Department of the Environment planned to list the building after the August Bank Holiday weekend in 1980, the company immediately demolished the art deco facade, leaving only the gateway and perimeter fence (now listed!).

A couple of Wallis, Gilbert and Partners buildings survive opposite the Firestone site. The **Pyrene Factory** was built for another American company, this time specialising in fire extinguishers. The design for this building marked the first time a central tower was used, by Wallis, Gilbert and Partners or possibly by anyone else in an interwar factory. The tower created a grand entrance with a staircase leading up to a decorated double doorway. The tower also had a functional use, with the company's technical drawing room situated at the top, with natural light provided from all sides. Pyrene left the factory in 1969 and it was converted to office use, with much of the decoration stripped away.

Pyrene Factory

Just along the road to the west is the former **Coty Cosmetics Factory** from 1932. Smaller in scale than the Firestone or Pyrene, nevertheless the Coty building has a certain elegance, with its office block featuring a stream-lined entranceway and metal framed, corner windows. Behind, the functional manufacturing buildings have now been demolished. The two-storey front building is constructed of reinforced concrete, using the Truscon method, with storage areas on the ground floor and offices on the first. The building is now home to a private health clinic, and an extra floor has been added.

Beyond the junction with Syon Lane is another Wallis, Gilbert & Partners design, this time a chemical factory for *Sir William Burnett & Co* (1933). Another small scale building, the factory was fitted into an awkwardly-shaped plot that approaches the road at a diagonal. The front building is low and streamlined, with a two storey section at the western end. The building is still standing for now, and home to a clothing company.

Coty Cosmetics Factory

Back down the eastern end of the Great West Road is Wallis, Gilbert & Partners biggest building in the area, the **Simmonds Aerocessories** plant, now known as Wallis House. In plan it is much like the slab and podium designs of many 1960s office blocks, which would later appear on the arterial roads, with an eleven storey tower rising above a lower range of buildings which feature small corner towers. The plot originally featured a small factory built by John Laing & Son Ltd. which was extended from 1937 through to 1942. The building is more in the mould of the Glaxo factory in Greenford, with its brick and stone finish. The building was provided with a large air raid shelter, complete with an operating theatre and hospital facilities. Simmonds left after World War II, and the building was occupied by the British Overseas Airways Company, who converted the whole premises to offices. It was later home to Glaxo SmithKilne, before being converted to apartments.

Simmonds Aerocessories

Of course other architects designed factories along the Great West Road in the interwar years. One of the best examples of art deco factory design of the 1930s is the former **Curry's Warehouse**, designed in 1936 by F.E Simpkins. Neighbour to the Pyrene factory, Curry's consists of a three-storey building with streamlined curves, metal-framed windows and a central clocktower. The building was used by Curry's, who at that time dealt in a variety of goods from bicycles to radios, as a distribution centre for their chain of shops. As with many of the other factories along this stretch of road, the building is now home to offices and has been kept in immaculate condition.

Back at the junction with Syon Lane is the **Gillette Factory** (1937), designed by the eminent Sir Banister Fletcher, architect, historian and barrister. Built for the American razor company, Fletcher used the same plan as found with many of the other Golden Mile buildings; a two storey block in brick with a horizontal arrangement of windows framed with metal surrounds, and a tall tower, originally faced on each side with a neon clock. Outside the main entrance are four sets of Victorian-era gas lamps and further down, a K6 telephone booth (designed by Sir Giles Gilbert Scott), setting a nice contrast with the brick functionalism of the factory. Gillette left the building in 2006, and in 2013 it was purchased to be converted into film studios, with additional facilities due to be complete by 2026.

Curry's Warehouse

Gillette Factory

Further west, next to the M4 which begins at Brentford as it splits from the Great West Road, is the town of Hayes, home to a number of factories and industrial buildings from the interwar years. The largest group belongs to what was the **EMI Factory** (1927-30) complex, a combination of buildings used for the manufacturing and distribution of records. The 50 acre site next to the railway had been purchased by the Gramophone Company, who would become EMI in 1930 after a merger, in 1906, with the Owen Williams-designed Gramophone Building on Blyth Road, built in 1912. 15 years later, Wallis, Gilbert and Partners were tasked with modernising the site, designing an extension to the Cabinet building, and a new Record store and a Shipping building, as well as other extensions. The new buildings were designed in an elegant art deco style, with none of the overt decoration of the Hoover or Firestone buildings.

The Cabinet building dates from 1916, built in a similar Truscon-constructed plan and style to the 1912 Gramophone Building. Wallis, Gilbert & Partners extended the building, using a square plan with deco corner towers and a connected bridge to the newly-built Shipping building. The Shipping building is rectangular in plan with long horizontal windows strips. The finished building is only a quarter of the size of the planned structure, with the intended extensions up to 950 ft, cancelled. The third building is the Record Store, a six storey building in reinforced concrete which tapers to a wedge shape on its awkward plot. Production moved from the site in 1978, and it was eventually sold and redeveloped as The Old Vinyl Factory apartments and offices.

EMI Record Store

Shipping Building

Record Store

Of course the new arterial roads took the driver out of the confines of London, and a number of factories and industrial buildings can be found just to the north in Hertfordshire. At Stirling Corner on the edge of Boreham-wood, is the former **Royal National Lifeboat Institute Warehouse**, now a storage facility. It was opened in 1939 as the RNLI moved their storage facilities from Poplar to Herts. The new building was designed by Herbert Kenchington in a suitably nautical fashion with a streamlined staircase tower and a long, low main building. As well as storage, the building contained workshops for manufacturing and repair, as well as offices, accommodation and an air raid shelter. The warehouse originally had bare yellow stock brick, now rendered white.

Further along the M1, we find a trio of factories at Hatfield and Welwyn. The **De Havilland Aviation Company** moved to Hatfield from Edgware in 1930 as the suburbs began to surround the Stag Lane aerodrome. In 1934 the facilities were upgraded with a factory, flying school and office buildings designed by architect Geoffrey Monro. The main surviving 1930s building is the office block, facing onto the road now known as Comet Way. It is a long 2-storey block with streamlined ranges that curves into the central entrance-way, marked by a small tower and featuring a reflecting pool in front. The building is constructed of white rendered reinforced concrete, with long strips of horizontal window bands and green tilework. To the south of this are the former staff mess and the gatehouse, both from 1934, and built in a similar streamlined fashion. The aerodrome closed in 1993, and the buildings are now occupied by the police and magistrates.

RNLI Warehouse

De Havilland Aircraft Factory

Just up the road in Welwyn Garden City are two factories that are among the most starkly modernist interwar examples in the country. The **Shredded Wheat Factory** opened in 1925, situated in the industrial zone of this planned town. It was designed by the architect-in-chief of the Garden City, Louis De Soissons and one of his assistants, A.W. Kenyon. Unlike the polite Neo-Georgian design of the rest of the town, the Shredded Wheat factory is a monolithic modernist structure in concrete and glass, dominated by the nine cylindrical double silos used to store the wheat. The factory was extended over the years, as the company expanded the works before closing in 2008. The site was bought for redevelopment with the later buildings cleared away. However the rebuilding of the site has yet to occur with the 1925 buildings still waiting for a new purpose.

The rest of this industrial area featured other interwar factories, among them one designed by Wallis, Gilbert & Partners for Young, Osmond and Young Heaters, now demolished. One other survivor is the **Roche Products Factory**, opened in 1940 and designed by Swiss architect Otto Salvisberg with C. Stanley Brown. The Roche building forgoes the art deco fripperies seen elsewhere, using the rationalist approach of mid-Europe with its starkly linear arrangement. The steel framed, reinforced concrete constructed office building presents its short end to Broadwater Road, the entrance accessed underneath an overhanging first floor supported by thin pilotis with a glass brick encased staircase to the side. To the rear at a 90 degree angle is a four storey factory block with metal casement windows and an off-white rendered finish. The building has now been converted into apartments and offices, and refurbished from the dilapidated state it had fallen into.

Shredded Wheat Factory

Roche Products Factory

In Kings Langley in the west of the county is the former **Ovaltine Factory**, an early art deco design for A.Wander Ltd, manufacturers of the drink, who had based themselves here in 1913. Based next to the Grand Union Canal, the original factory from 1923 was a long three storey block in stone with large windows, with extensions throughout the 1920s in a similar style, all by J.A. Bowden. Bowden also designed the local Diary and Poultry farms to supply the factory, although these were built in a historical style, based on a farm built by Louis XVI for Queen Marie Antoinette. Ovaltine stopped production here in 2002 and both the factory extension and the dairy farm have now been converted to housing.

The town of Watford was known for its print industry in the first half of the 20th century, with a number of printworks around the vicinity, often designed by modernist architects. The sole remaining fragment of this once thriving industry is the pump station and clock tower to the **Sun Factory Substation** on Ascot Road. The large factory premises were built in 1934, designed by George W. Knight of Stanley Peach & Partners. The clock tower is towards the arts and crafts end of the art deco spectrum, built in white rendered walls, green pan tiled roof and 'SUN' spelled out in geometric letters on the small tower. The locally listed structure has laid dormant for some years waiting to be reused.

To the north of the town stood two other architecturally interesting printworks; Odhams Press and Ault & Wiborg. The Odhams Press works was designed by Owen Williams between 1935-8, with a functional, reinforced concrete two storey building. A Press Hall was added in 1954 by Yates, Cook & Darbyshire with a Scandinavian influenced clock tower. The earlier building was demolished and the later one turned into a supermarket. Opposite was the Ault & Wiborg site, designed by Wallis, Gilbert & Partners in 1936, to supply ink to the Odhams Press. It had a two storey 170 ft frontage with a curved entrance way and two storage sheds behind. The factory was demolished in 2007.

Ovaltine Factory

Sun Printers Substation, Watford